# Alliter_____ Alphabet

A fun way to teach preliteracy skills to kids!

written by Taralee A. O'Malley-Hurff & Heather A. Grim

TAOH Inspired Education, LLC
Printed in the U.S.A.
www.taohinspirededucation.com

## TARALEE
### O'MALLEY · HURFF

Copyright© 2015 TAOH Inspired Education, LLC
Printed in the United States of America

Library of Congress Control Number: 2015917740

All rights reserved. Permission is granted for the user to reproduce the material contained herein in limited form for classroom or homeschooling use only. Reproduction of this material for an entire class, school, school system, or homeschooling co-op is strictly prohibited. A reviewer may quote brief passages in a review to be printed in a magazine, newspaper or on the Web with permission in writing from one of the authors. For additional information about permissions, please email taohinspirededucation@gmail.com.

Edited by Ruby Andrescavage

Design and text layout by Margaret Cogswell
www.spiderbuddydesigns.com

*This book is dedicated to all of our students who inspired us and challenged us to be better teachers!*

## Special Acknowledgments

To my children...Harrison, Jackson and Teagan...I am so grateful for all of your insight throughout the creative process that brought *Alliteration Alphabet* to life! Your enthusiasm and support make me believe I can do anything!!! You are the light that brightens every one of my days.
— Taralee A. O'Malley-Hurff

To my boys...Your laughs and genuine spirits have inspired me to be the light to others that you are to me. I have especially enjoyed sharing the creation of *Alliteration Alphabet* with you, as it was a wonderful project for us to share as a family. To my family, words are not enough to express the gratitude I have. I thank God every day for all the wonderful moments and for you in my life.
— Heather A. Grim

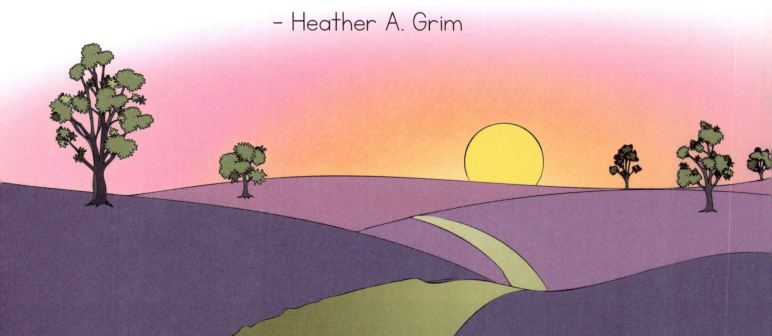

# Using Your Alliteration Alphabet Book

Let's dive in and talk about how you can use *Alliteration Alphabet* in your classroom or home! Taralee and Heather will provide you with some insight on how they taught the contents; and, at the end of the book, you will find some fabulous resources to help you expand your lessons and activities even further. *Alliteration Alphabet* has a page dedicated to each letter of the alphabet. You will see the uppercase and lowercase letter represented and color coded, each with a tracing line. The poems are in the center of the page with corresponding illustrations surrounding the text.

In the classroom, the poems and content of *Alliteration Alphabet* have been taught in different ways. One approach teaches the letters in developmental acquisition order (p/b, t/d, k/g, f/v, s/z, m/n, w/h, l/r, y/j, c/q, x…a/e/i/o/u) whereas the other uses straight line letters followed by curvy letters. This exemplifies how you can use *Alliteration Alphabet* in different ways to meet the needs of varied learners.

Suggested materials are as follows. Remember, these are merely suggestions and you will have to adjust your approach in order to meet the needs of your child or students.

- » Pencil (Taralee and Heather love to use golf pencils with their students. Using a golf pencil will encourage a tripod grasp and they are more manageable for little hands.)
- » Highlighters in **blue** and **yellow** (You can also use markers, colored pencils, etc.)
- » Crayons

# Ideas for Instruction

**1.** For parents, you will want to sit with your child and work on the book together. Look at it as an investment of quality time and a fun learning experience.

For educators, a small group setting is recommended, but it can be adapted for a whole group presentation as well.

**2.** Introduce the letter you are working on, pointing out both the uppercase and lowercase letters. If appropriate, have the children trace the letters, following your example.*

**3.** Explain how you are going to look for the target letter in the uppercase and lowercase form throughout. Tell the children to act like a detective as you read.

**4.** Read the text to the children. When you finish, go through to find all the uppercase target letters and then the lowercase target letters. This is where you will have the students use the highlighters. Be sure to make this interactive. Have the children show you the target letters and make the mark on the letter. You can practice the letter sound as you find them as well.

**5.** Finally, you will find the alliterative words and match them to the illustrations. Have the children color in the illustrations.

*Both educators used the Handwriting Without Tears curriculum to teach the letter formations and prewriting skills. You can find out more about this curriculum at www.hwtears.com.

To enhance motivation and engagement, a plush mascot can be used for each letter. Children enjoy objects that match the illustrations, and it will help them continue to connect the preliteracy skills to their environment.

# Aa

Amy Alligator likes to eat apples and acorns. Amy Alligator also likes to watch airplanes fly by all day long.

6

# B b

Billy Bear likes to ride his bike near the beach. Billy Bear enjoys taking a bath before he goes to bed.

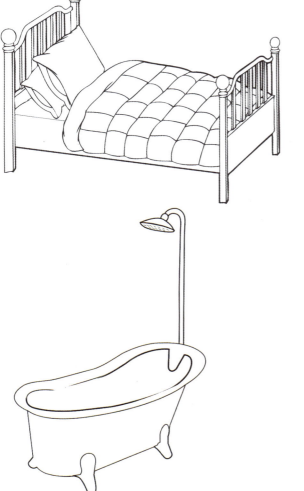

# Cc

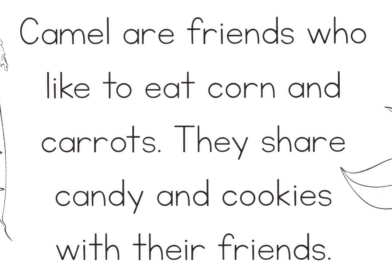

Connie Cow and Carlos Camel are friends who like to eat corn and carrots. They share candy and cookies with their friends.

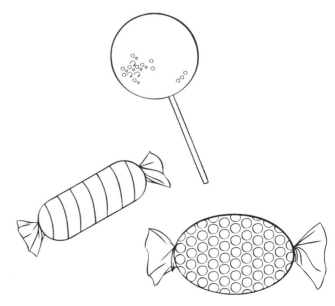

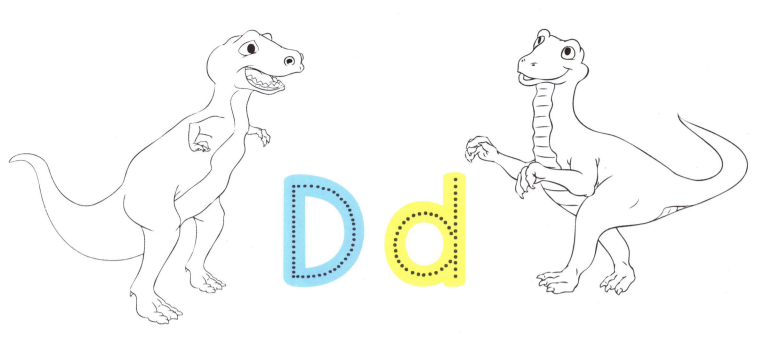

# Dd

Danny Dinosaur likes to dig in the dirt, dance with his Dad and get his teeth cleaned by the dentist.

Ernie Elephant eats eleven eggs for breakfast. Ernie Elephant enjoys exercising early in the morning.

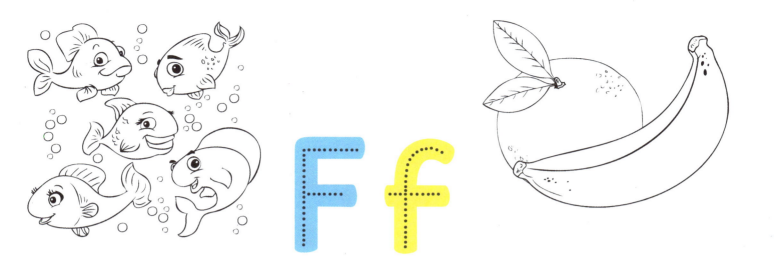

# F f

Freddie Frog lives near a farm. Freddie Frog swims with five fish in the pond. Freddie Frog eats flies and fruit.

# Gg

Gordon Goat likes to gobble green grapes with his friend Gloria Goose. Gordon Goat and Gloria Goose play games on the grass.

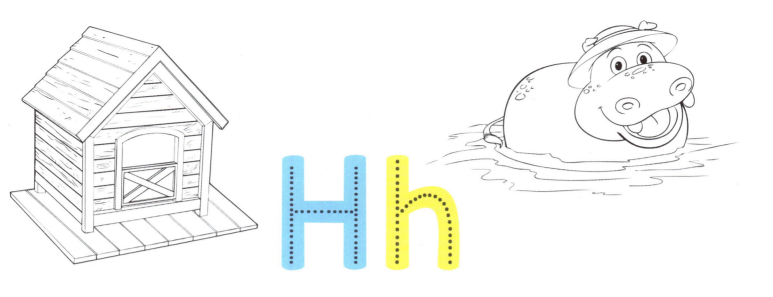

# Hh

Harrison Horse likes to eat hay by his house. His friend Hunter Hippo wears a hat and floats in the water when it is hot.

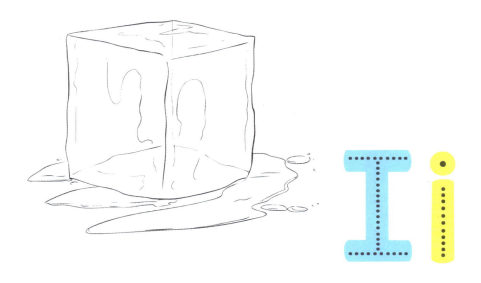

# I i

Izzy Iguana eats insects and ice cubes in the summer.

Jackson Jaguar jumps in the jungle. Jackson Jaguar likes to eat jelly beans and Jell-O®.

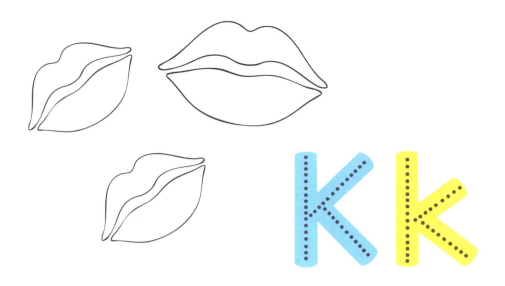

Kelly Kangaroo kisses her kid Kingston. Kingston likes to fly his kite and pretend to be a king.

Larry Lion lounges by the lake.
His friend Lucy Ladybug likes
to lay on the leaves.

# Mm

Marco Moose munches muffins and drinks milk in the moonlight.

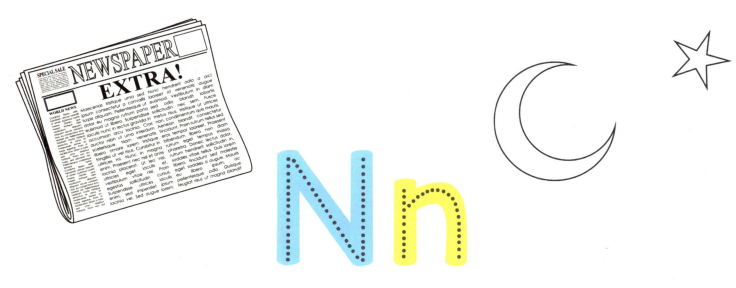

# Nn

Nancy Nightingale sits in her nest practicing numbers at night. Nancy Nightingale eats noodles and reads the newspaper.

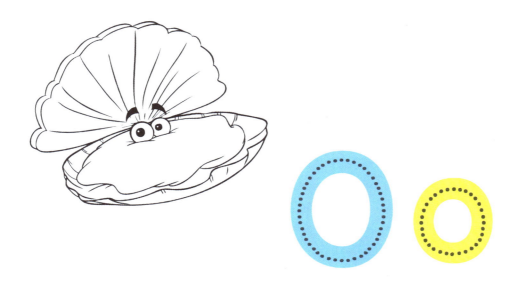

Olivia Octopus loves the color orange. Olivia Octopus plays in the ocean with an old oyster named Oscar.

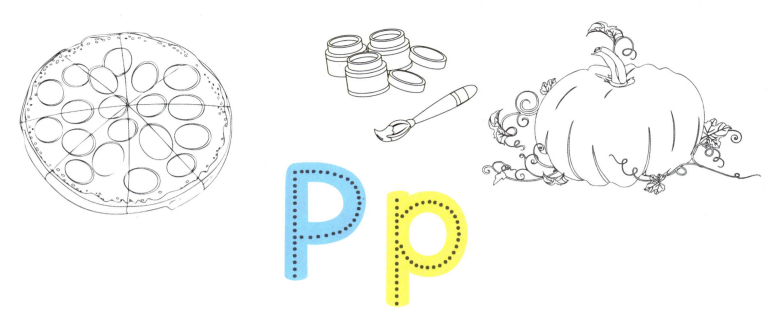

# P p

Penelope Pig likes to eat pepperoni pizza and popcorn while she paints pumpkins in the park.

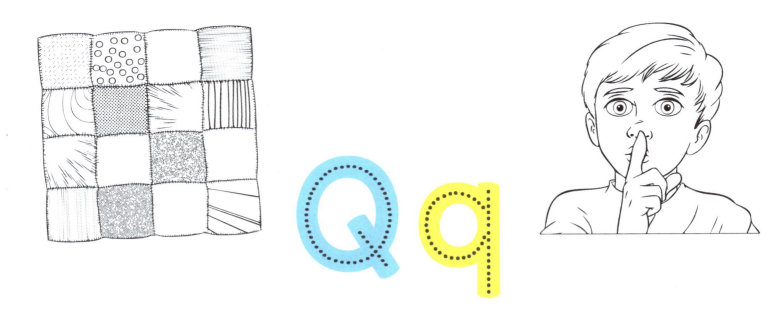

Quinton Quail and Queen Quintella like to make quilts and play quietly.

# Rr

Ruby Rabbit hops on the rocks in the grass. Ruby Rabbit likes to look for rainbows after it rains.

Sebastian Seal likes to spin the soccer ball on his nose. Sebastian Seal likes to sit in the sun and watch the sailboats go by.

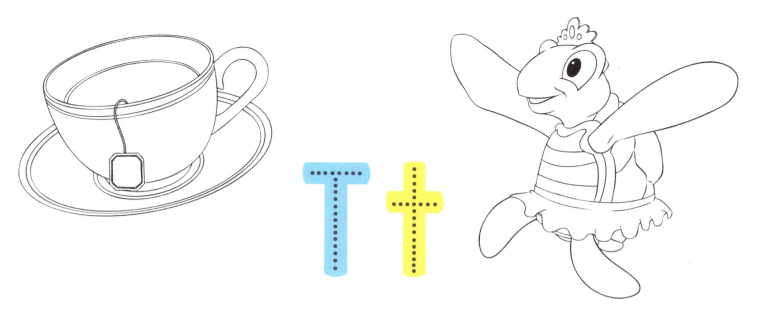

Teagan Turtle likes to wear her
tiara and tutu while drinking tea.
Her friend Tanner Turkey
loves to eat tacos and
tell time for the town.

Ulanie Unicorn plays her ukulele while upstairs under her umbrella.

Vicky Violet plays her violin while using her voice to sing to the vegetables.

# W w

Wanda Whale whistles a tune while Walter Walrus makes a wish.

# Xx

Mr. Bones has an extra special job to take x-rays. Mr. Bones uses the x-rays to explain about our bones.

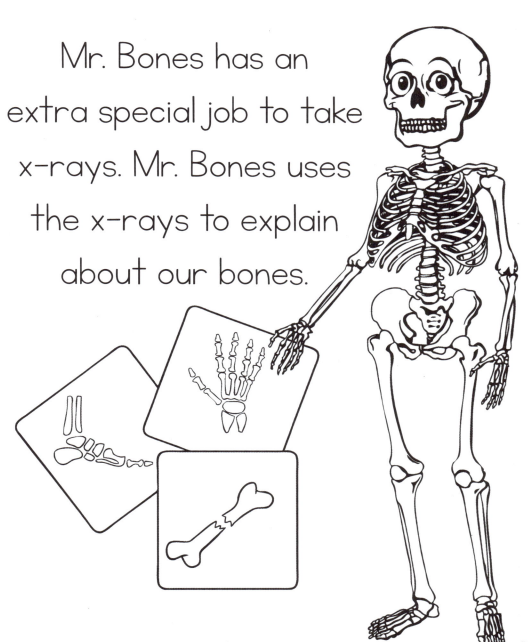

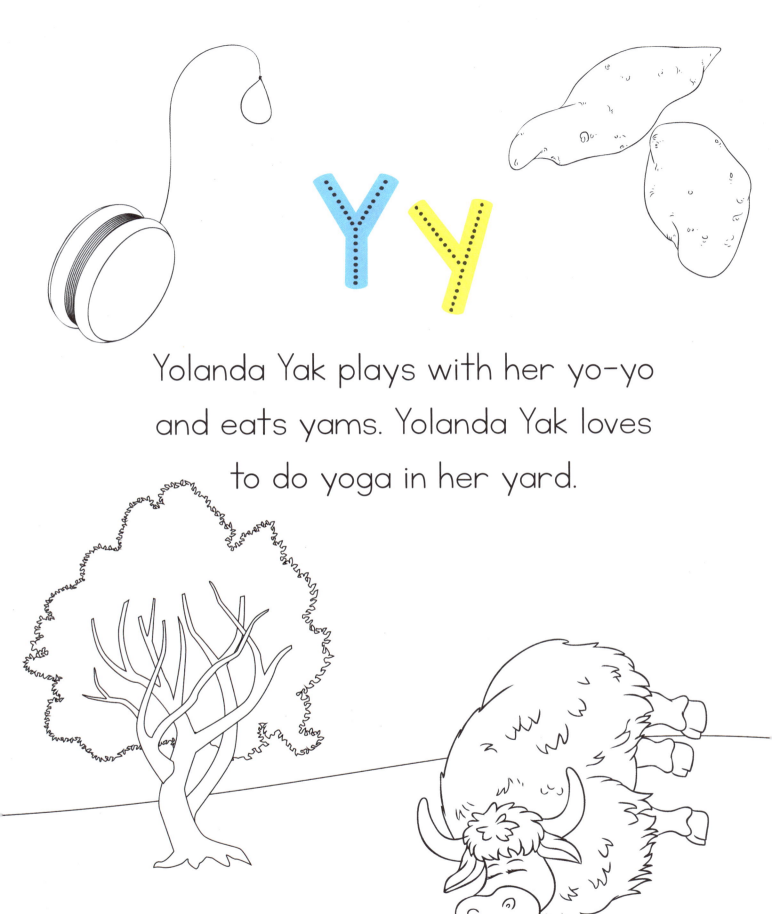

# Y y

Yolanda Yak plays with her yo-yo and eats yams. Yolanda Yak loves to do yoga in her yard.

Zoe Zebra lives in the zoo, zips her jacket and loves zuchinni.

# Alphabet Themes & Topics

Educators use themes or topics to develop lessons and engage learners. This is an especially successful and exciting method for teaching young learners. The idea of using themes or topics can be used in the home or in school settings. Theme or topic choices can be traditional or nontraditional.

Let creativity and the interest of your learners guide your choices. You can even use the letter you are learning about to assist in guiding your theme or topic choice. Use centers such as art, science, math, dramatic play, writing, reading (or library), cooking and sensory table to explore, discover and learn. Hands-on activities will bring your classroom to life!

## Aa
animals
apples
aliens

## Bb
balls
birds
bugs

## Cc
clouds
caterpillars
clocks

## Dd
dirt
day
dance

## Ee
eyes
emotions
environment

## Ff
fish
feel & fingers
fruit

## Gg
grow
games
garden

## Hh
hats
houses
holidays

## Ii
I-Spy
ice
inventions

## Jj
jars
jungle
jellyfish

## Kk
kitchen
keys
kites

## Ll
LEGO® blocks
leaves
ladybugs

## Mm
movement
mazes
monsters

## Nn
noodles
night
nose (smell)

## Oo
obstacles
opposites
Olympics

## Pp
puppets
poems
playdough

## Qq
questions
quiet
quilts

## Rr
races
rainbows
rhyming words

## Ss
stars & stripes
seasons
school

## Tt
toys
teeth
tools

## Uu
underwater
USA
umbrellas

## Vv
vehicles
vegetables
volcanoes

## Ww
worms
wet
weather

## Xx
x-rays
x marks the spot
bo<u>x</u>

## Yy
yummy & yucky
yarn
yoga

## Zz
zippers
zoos
zig-zags

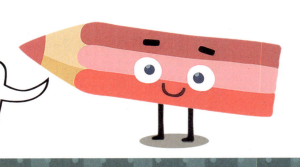

Here are some excellent ideas to get you started!

# Big Letter Activities

Using the letter of the alphabet that you are teaching with a tangible association project will further reinforce preliteracy skills and understanding letter use with everyday objects. For this activity you will need a large letter cutout for each child (8.5x11" or 11x14" size works best), as well as the supplies for decorating the letter.

Here are some creative ideas for decorating your BIG letters!

**Aa**: apple prints; animal tracks; ants (make with fingerprints)
**Bb**: buttons; beans; bubble wrap
**Cc**: colored corn; cotton balls; candy
**Dd**: dirt; dots; doodles
**Ee**: eyes (wiggle eyes); elbow macaroni; emotion pictures
**Ff**: feathers; flowers; fingerprints
**Gg**: glitter; glue; grass
**Hh**: hearts; holes (use a hole puncher); hay

**Ii**: ink (use with stamps); paint with ice; insects

**Jj**: jewels; jellyfish; jelly beans

**Kk**: Kix cereal; kites; kisses (lip marks)

**Ll**: letters; leaves; lollipops

**Mm**: money; marshmallows; maps

**Nn**: noodles; newspaper; nocturnal animals

**Oo**: oats; Os (like the Olympic rings); pictures of opposites

**Pp**: popcorn; puzzle pieces; pipe cleaners

**Qq**: Q-tips® painting; quilt (have each child decorate a square and put together as a class quilt); question marks

**Rr**: rice; rainbows; rhyming words

**Ss**: stickers; stamps; stencils

**Tt**: tissue paper; tissues; tape (decorative tape would be fun)

**Uu**: umbrellas; decorate the U with things that live underwater; glue pictures upside down

**Vv**: velvet pieces; Valentines; Velcro®

**Ww**: shredded wheat; paint with water colors; weather pictures

**Xx**: Xs for X-marks the spot; pictures of things that end in X (box, fox, ox)

**Yy**: yarn; yellow; pictures of yoga poses

**Zz**: draw or trace zig-zags; zoo animals; decorate the Z with the words "zip" and "zap"

# Recommended Reading

Teaching children new concepts requires a lot of reinforcement and repetition. Shared reading with your child or students is a perfect time to pick fun and engaging books! We have compiled a reading list to get you started using alliteration and repetition to expose children to preliteracy skills.

**Aa**: *All The Awake Animals Are Almost Asleep* by Crescent Dragonwagon

**Bb**: *Bootsie Barker Bites* by Barbara Bottner

**Cc**: *Click, Clack, Moo: Cows That Type* by Doreen Cronin

**Dd**: *Drumheller Dinosaur Dance* by Robert Heidbreder

**Ee**: *Ella the Elegant Elephant* by Carmela D'amico and Steven D'amico

**Ff**: *Four Famished Foxes and Fosdyke* by Pamela Duncan Edwards

**Gg**: *The Three Billy Goats Gruff* by Ellen Appleby

**Hh**: *My Hippo Has The Hiccups: And Other Poems I Totally Made Up (A Poetry Speaks Experience)* by Kenn Nesbitt

**Ii**: *"If..." series* by Laura Numeroff
**Jj**: *Jamberry* by Bruce Degen
**Kk**: *K is for Kissing a Cool Kangaroo* by Giles Andreae
**Ll**: *Llama, Llama Red Pajama* by Anna Dewdney
**Mm**: *The Recess Queen* by Alexis O'Neill
**Nn**: *Nelly, That's Not Nice!* by Ruth Lerner Pearle
**Oo**: *Commotion in the Ocean* by Giles Andreae
**Pp**: *Lilly's Purple Plastic Purse* by Kevin Henkes
**Qq**: *Quiet! There's A Canary in the Library* by Don Freeman
**Rr**: *The Little Mouse, the Red Ripe Strawberry, and the Big Hungry Bear* by Don Wood and Audrey Wood
**Ss**: *The Spaghetti-Slurping Sewer Serpent* by Laura Ripes
**Tt**: *In the Tall, Tall Grass* by Denise Fleming
**Uu**: *Aliens Love Underpants!* by Claire Freedman
**Vv**: *Vulture View* by April Pulley Sayre
**Ww**: *Mrs. Wishy-Washy* by Joy Cowley
**Xx**: *My Mom Has X-Ray Vision* by Angela McAllister
**Yy**: *The Yak Who Yelled Yuck* by Carol Pugliano-Martin
**Zz**: *Zany Zebras* by Nancy Parent

Reading aloud helps build word-sound awareness.

# About the Authors

### Taralee A. O'Malley-Hurff

Taralee is an educator, philanthropist and a published author. Her book, *100 Things To Do Before You Are 10*, is the go-to resource for family bonding and adventure. Taralee has passionately contributed to the fields of special education and early childhood education since 1998, meeting with her students as needed in the home or in school. She excels at recognizing every child's unique gift and successfully ignites their love of learning through exploration, discovery and play. It is through this work that Inspired Education was born. As a philanthropist, Taralee currently serves as the President of the Board of Trustees for the Southern Regional New Jersey Early Intervention Collaborative, and she's in her seventh year as a Board Member. Taralee enjoys family life in Southern New Jersey with her husband and three children. Find out more about Taralee by visiting her website at: www.taohinspirededucation.com.

## Heather A. Grim

Heather is the Supervisor of Student Services in Early Intervention at the Berks County Intermediate Unit in Berks County, PA. She has worked at the Intermediate Unit for the last 14 years and has been in her current position for the last four years. Her heart continues to be in educating children during their preschool years, and in her position she is able to work with staff to determine some of the best ways to program for children. She enjoys supporting staff with programming and works with administration to support program growth and needs. Heather also is a certified Safety Care Instructor and supports behavior trainings for the Early Intervention program. Heather is a mom of two busy boys, Hunter and Tanner ages 12 and 8, and a very large Rottweiler named Diesel. Her boys, their sports, and her wonderful extensive family keep her busy and loving life.

# Praise for Alliteration Alphabet

"*Alliteration Alphabet* by Taralee O'Malley-Hurff and Heather Grim is both a fun and appropriate text to use with pre-emerging readers. This high interest book for early learners provides print awareness, phonological awareness, vocabulary, and narrative skills while providing a platform for letter knowledge in a multisensory format — all quality details in promoting early literacy skills!"

Kristine Rosenberger

Ed.D., Director of Curriculum and Instruction, Shillington, PA

"*Alliteration Alphabet* will delight children and help them build the relationship between letter and sound. This book presents complicated concepts in a direct and enjoyable manner. The helpful strategies for classroom or home use are invaluable. This is a book a child will want to pick up again and again."

Carolyn Miller

M.A., M.Ed Principal & Administrative Dean

"A fun and active resource for teachers, parents and children to learn about preliteracy! This book engages children in learning and playing with literacy and provides parents and teachers with awesome resources to make literacy fun! I'm recommending this book to my colleagues, friends and family."

Cheri L. Woyurka

Director of Early Childhood and Student Services

**For more information and free downloads, visit www.taohinspirededucation.com.**